Where is Little Softy?

Written by Catherine Baker
Illustrated by JiaJia Hamner

Collins

2

3

4

6

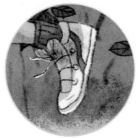

10

What happened to Little Softy?

🐾 Review: After reading 🐾

Read 1: Phonemic awareness

- Play 'find it!' by looking for the items in the small circles at the bottom of the pages, to build phonemic awareness. Choose an object or two per page and ask the children to find them in the illustration. Emphasise the initial sound of each word and then say the word. (e.g. Can you find a ddd duck?)
- When they have found the object, ask the children to say the first sound of the word.
- Look at pages 14 and 15 together and ask the children to retell what happens in the book. Can they find each of the pictures in the book?

Read 2: Vocabulary

- Encourage the children to hold the book and turn the pages.
- Spend time looking at the pictures and discussing them, drawing on any relevant experience or knowledge the children have. Encourage them to talk about what they can see in each picture, giving as much detail as they can. Expand the children's vocabulary by naming objects in the illustrations that they do not know.
- Sound-talk an object or two from the circles at the bottom of each page. (e.g. Can you find the c-a-t?) Sound-talk but do not blend the word. When the children find the object, encourage them to blend the word.

Read 3: Comprehension

- Read the book again. Ask:
    - o Where was Little Softy at the beginning of the story?
    - o Does the story have a happy ending? What happens?